A REASSESSMENT OF US COUNTER-DRUG STRATEGY AND POLICY

Illicit drugs undermine cultural values, degrade people, damage societies, and destroy governments. A drug dependent America can neither continue to lead through the 21st century nor continue to provide the promise of opportunity to future generations.

> The first duty of government is to protect its citizens. The Constitution of the United States – as interpreted over 208 years – articulates the obligation of the federal government to uphold the public good, providing a bulwark against all threats, foreign and domestic. Illegal drugs constitute one such threat. Toxic, addictive substances present a hazard to society as a whole. Like a corrosive, insidious cancer, drug abuse diminishes the potential of our citizens for full growth and development.[1]

The economist Ludwig von Mises postulated, "Once the principle is admitted that it is the duty of government to protect the individual against his own foolishness, no serious objection can be advanced against further encroachments."[2]

Herein lays the political dilemma - a democratic paradox. The threat of drugs is well recognized, as is the obligation of a government to safeguard its population. But to what extent can a democratic government rightfully protect a society from itself and still be a democracy? The manner in which a democratic government responds to the threat of drugs is a natural point of contention that often obscures focus and fractures the unity essential to a lasting success. Various approaches, methods, and strategies: enforcement, treatment, education, harm reduction, and legalization reflect societies' differing opinions on the proper role of a democratic government. That there is disagreement by the people, in a government of the people, is only natural, but the disagreement must not so encumber government that it effectively ceases to govern.

> The rule of law and individual freedom are not incompatible. Although government must minimize interference in the private lives of citizens, it cannot deny people the security on which peace of mind depends. Drug abuse impairs rational thinking and the potential for a full, productive life. Drug abuse, drug trafficking, and their consequences destroy personal liberty and the well-being of communities. Drugs drain the physical, intellectual, spiritual, and moral strength of America. Crime, violence, workplace accidents, family misery, drug-exposed children, and addiction are only part of the price imposed on society. Illegal drugs indiscriminately destroy old and young, men and women, from all racial and ethnic groups and every walk of life.[3]

Background

"Pharmacology is older than agriculture." "The use of drugs ....can be traced back to mans' early history."[4] Indeed, the War on Drugs (WoD) has taken many names and forms, but today it exists in an environment that causes more rapid and widespread effects. A look at the nature of the problem is a logical first step in analysis. To find a benchmark, one needs to look no further than 20th century American history. This paper revisits the lessons of current history, assesses the impacts of current policy and strategy, considers the relationship between policy and strategy, and ultimately proposes a better way forward.

History

In 1914, the first federal law was passed regarding narcotics. The Harrison Act "established a very modest 'sin tax' on the sale of narcotics such as opiates."[5] Individuals willing to break the law realized the lucrative opportunities this new environment created and began smuggling narcotics. Government action to control and tax social behaviors facilitated rapid and profitable criminal exploitation. By the time the 18th Amendment to the Constitution (Prohibition, 1920) and the Marijuana Tax Act (1937) were passed, bootleggers, moon-shiners, rumrunners, dealers, pushers and gangsters had fine-tuned the black market trade and learned to violently protect their businesses. A new era of crime, violence, and corruption had been created by the law intended to protect society.

Passage of the 18th Amendment brought robust opportunities to lower-level criminals and mobsters that would otherwise not have occurred. It fostered criminal cooperation, created incentive to organize criminal structures, and provided lucrative rewards. Subsequent repeal of Prohibition in 1933 enticed criminal migration into narcotics. Although the League of Nations created treaties aimed at curtailing illicit trafficking, the years after WWII bore witness to a strong resurgence in the international drug trade. The Italian Mafia established the "French Connection" and dominated the heroin trade for decades, supplying 95% of US demand for the drug and opening the United States to international organized crime. In Asia, Chiang Kai-Shek turned to opium as a way to resource his army after he was deposed[6] and soon the "Golden Triangle" became the world supplier of opium. As a result, "…the politics of Southeast Asia became more chaotic, more gangs sprang up to challenge governments, turning to opium for money and finally becoming very little different from bands of smugglers."[7]

Policy Focus

Values have played a critical role in the escalation of drug use and the evolution of US drug policy. The counter-culture of the 1960's formed its own values and rejected the traditions of mainstream America. Drugs were integral to this new lifestyle and … "[t]he huge demand for illegal drugs … created the conditions that allowed international drug trafficking to expand and flourish."[8] US demand caused the formation of powerful Latin American drug cartels and by the late 1960's, the cocaine market had transformed the drug from cost prohibitive to the drug of choice for the average user – an American epidemic had begun. Presidents Kennedy, Johnson, and Nixon dealt with the evolving problem primarily through law enforcement, increased agency authority, and source elimination. Although Presidents Ford and Carter largely continued the anti-drug policy, by 1980 the country had reaped little reward from the consistent hard-line anti-drug policy.[9]

Despite the failure, the Reagan Administration took on an even more robust posture and shepherded in the era of "The Drug Czar," "Zero Tolerance," and "Just Say No." The War on Drugs (WoD) was declared in 1982 and many countries became active in the fight against trafficking; a renewed international effort had begun.[10] The new efforts, backed by strong legislative support, led to massive increases in funding, increased agency authority, troop allocations, equipment procurement, and all-out efforts to keep drugs from crossing US borders. The WoD shifted into high gear, apparently lacking an appreciation for the peripheral effects of the effort, some of which Prohibition had foretold.

Public opinion polls revealed that Americans wanted their leadership to get even tougher regarding the deterrence of drug use and the elimination of the crime and violence that surrounds the drug culture. Congress supported public will and President George H. Bush pledged to continue the WoD. Although candidate Bill Clinton promised to change US policy, Uncle Sam continued to aggressively pursue the external aspects of the strategy; efforts were aimed at reducing the supply of drugs from source countries. The United States provided assistance and concurrently levied pressure on these countries to eliminate the problem within their borders; they were to eradicate crops, destroy processing labs, break-up drug rings, and interdict outgoing shipments.

The focus on existential causes for the drug problem continues today and resonates well with a domestic US audience. It points a finger of blame outside US borders, builds an inherent excuse for failure within US systems, and portrays US society as a victim of evil outside forces as opposed to an element of its own domestic problem. For politicians attempting to curry favor with voters through a tough stance on drugs, it is a safe and effective domestic message – but one that is heard by an international audience as well. The rise of globalization has increased the impact and visibility of the US policy message throughout the world – and it has not been well received by all members of the global community. Foreign countries view the US policy as interventionist and unfair, and stress that little is done within the United States to curb demand. Instead, blame is affixed to smaller, weaker source countries with fewer resources and less capability to deal with the problems. [11]

The Nature of the Problem

Historically, war tends to escalate, and pragmatically, there are no end-state objectives identified in the WoD. War is in fact a poor metaphor for the drug problem for a number of reasons. To Americans, it implies an end – a declared victory, surrender, and cessation of effort. However, it is the continuation of effort that is essential to success in anti-drug measures. As Steven Taylor of the Center for Contemporary Conflict stated, "…while underscoring the gravity of an issue may help galvanize political action, the invocation of the war analogy also presupposes a chance at victory. Hence, the double-edged nature of this type of rhetoric: these types of wars are often foreordained to be lost…"[12] The anticipated endstate never comes to fruition because any reduction in pressure facilitates continuation or resurgence. "There can be no short-term solutions to a problem that requires education of each generation and resolute opposition to criminal traffickers. Our approach must be long-term and continuous."[13] "The moment we believe ourselves to be victorious and free to relax our resolve, drug abuse will rise again."[14]

Indeed, drug use appears to be cyclic in nature, the ebb and flow resulting from the response of an unaware public to the sudden revelation of a drug problem within their society,[15] and their subsequent inattention after the problem has been subdued. The relaxation of effort in countering the threat of drugs eventually results in a resurgence of the problem. Thus, policy effort must be enduring and insomuch as it is enduring, policy must be acceptable to the public. The public will is essential to any enduring policy.

The politics of the issue, the need to maintain pressure on the drug problem, and the role of political rhetoric have, to-date, made the status quo the most acceptable policy option. The reality of political fear, political self interest, and public ignorance weigh heavily on the domestic policy message. Given these realities, the prime importance has not been effectiveness of policy, but the fact that the policy message resonates with the public. This remains the surest way for politicians to ensure continuity of effort, manage public perception, and maintain public support. The linkage between continuity of policy, acceptability of the policy message and political fear is irrefutable, and in this instance, paradoxical as well.

Policy has painted anti-drug efforts as being on par with war, which implies an all out effort to achieve victory and a subsequent condition of peace. Yet, the cyclical nature of the drug problem requires a continuity of effort to keep it under control. It should come as no surprise that this paradox has polarized the way society views the solution. One view demands an all out fight against the evils of drugs, while the other believes the fight is what causes most of the adverse effects. The United States is engaged in what is necessarily a prolonged effort but is encumbered by a significant lack of internal unity. History clearly illustrates that Americans will not support a never-ending "war" that yields no lasting results and shows little promise of success.

Peripheral Impacts

Given the corruption and violence that Prohibition caused in an established democracy, one would naturally expect the effects on transitioning democracies to be much more severe. These newer governments lack the mature institutions and the architecture of a developed civil society that helps manage complex challenges. Although results from US efforts during Prohibition can be extrapolated, policy makers seem to have neither considered these results nor drawn analogies to the current WoD. The numerous second and third order effects that are unpleasant for the United States have proven to be devastating in countries with developing democracies. The crime, corruption, disorder, violence, financial costs, medical impacts, linkage to poverty, and support to narco-terrorist groups are just some of the adverse peripheral effects of drug use, drug policy, and the WoD. These peripheral effects undermine the legitimate governments of these developing nations and threaten their survival, thus magnifying the detrimental effects on US national security strategy.

Crime

In 1920 social scientists, politicians, and clergy determined that alcohol consumption was a major cause of societal problems. They believed that if alcohol was removed from society, "crime and corruption would decrease, poverty would be abated, tax burdens created by prisons and poor houses would be reduced, and health and hygiene" would improve.[16] As history has shown, not only were these lofty social aspirations never achieved, but the opposite effect was created. Prohibition did not remove alcohol from society - it merely required society to either break the law or abstain. Those who chose to break the law, and profit through illicit means, conducted business in a world devoid of the rule of law; there was no legislative, executive, or judicial branch to establish norms or maintain order.

Each illicit organization had to provide for its own protection and secure its own interests. Ultimately, the force that prevailed was and is the one capable of projecting the most violence. Homicide rates in the United States illustrate this point. The highest rates were in the years 1933 and 1980 – 1933 being the last year alcohol Prohibition was enforced and 1980 marking the escalation of drug enforcement efforts.[17]

According to Marina Maggessi, former Chief Inspector of Rio de Janeiro's Drug Repression Center, "Ninety percent of all crime today has drugs at the root." Drug gangs have turned Rio into one of the most violent cities in the world. "The homicide rate in Rio is around 50 per 100,000 people, compared to eight per 100,000 in New York City and three per 100,000 in London."[18]

In Mexico, the government's military response to violence was spurred by the public perception that the police were corrupt and organized crime was out of control.

> There were 2,100 drug-related murders last year, up from 1,300 in 2005. Some 600 killings took place in Michoacan alone in 2006. Many of the murders involved brutal cruelty: in a notorious case, five severed heads were dumped in a dance hall in Michoacan.[19]

Clearly, the drug trade is an excellent venue for groups and individuals with no regard or restraint for the use of violence.

Richard Cowan, a well-known activist for the legalization of marijuana, coined the phrase, "The Iron Law of Prohibition." Cowan describes the irony of the Prohibition rationale in that "the more intense the law enforcement, the more potent the prohibited substances became ..." the over-indulgences, crime, and injuries that resulted would not have occurred were there no legal restraints.[20] True to Cowan's rationale, crime and violence increased as people found ways to obtain alcohol, either by making it, stealing it, or buying it on the black market.

Corruption

Corruption is perhaps the most corrosive of all the peripheral effects on a functioning government. It serves as a catalyst that breaks down law and order, civil society, and the capabilities of even a fully functional government. The political and social aspects of corruption are difficult to manage, and the drug trade creates so much corruption that it pervades nearly every existing system.

To levy unfettered anti-drug cooperation in developing countries is nearly impossible, and when cooperation occurs, it is difficult to know for sure that it has. Interest often lies in undermining a competitor, establishing false trust within enforcement agencies, or maintaining the status quo rather than countering the drug trade. When Mexican President Felipe Caldron took office December 1, 2006, he turned to the army to bring under control what had been decades of police corruption. He quickly moved to "disarm the local police, confiscating their guns for ballistics tests to check whether they had been used in murders. Like many ill-paid local forces in Mexico, the Tijuana police are widely regarded as working for, rather than against, the drug mob.[21]

The large profits realized through the drug trade enables traffickers to entice officials from various countries to directly aid their operations or to look the other way while business is conducted. "Authorities believe that, in Venezuela, President Hugo Chavez turns a blind eye to trafficking by FARC guerrillas, 50 of whom were indicted last year by the United States on trafficking charges."[22] Estimates indicate that officials receive over $100 million in bribes from Columbian narcotics cartels every year.[23] The extent that corruption, greed, and bribery can influence justice and enforcement officials makes it exceedingly difficult for agents in many countries to conduct successful anti-drug operations. Even in the United States there are staggering numbers of public officials (police and government officials) who accept bribes and kickbacks as a regular part of doing business.[24] "On average, half of all police officers convicted as a result of FBI-led corruption cases between 1993 and 1997 were convicted for drug-related offenses."[25]

Poverty Trap

Illegal drugs "act as a terrible form of regressive tax – not only transferring wealth to an elite group of manufacturers but also robbing the poor underclass of the ability to generate income and savings and lead productive lives."[26] Due to the opportunity that the environment provides, "Drug dealing plays a substantial role in the local economies of poorer urban neighborhoods" and it serves to keep these communities in a state of poverty.[27] Drugs contribute to fear, corruption and increased levels of crime and violence in disadvantaged neighborhoods. These neighborhoods provide the perfect environment and are the dealers' location of choice for distribution centers.[28] A tragic mix is created with the immense potential profit, the deficit of legitimate opportunity, and the fact that drug dealers target these neighborhoods. The result is a snare that lures the less fortunate with the incentive of quick, easy, and lucrative profits.

Increased opportunity is a key component to defeating this element of the drug trade. Unfortunately, policy currently works in juxtaposition to increased opportunity. Enforcement measures eliminate educational opportunity for those who become entangled in the snare. If convicted of even a minor drug possession offense, a student can lose access to student loans, grants, and scholarships – under these conditions opportunity for education is severely curtailed if not eliminated.[29] For poor students, the loss of educational opportunity coupled with a drug offense can make rewarding legal employment exceedingly difficult to find. Thus their best opportunity may become the neighborhood and the trade they had hoped to escape. The lure of an easy profit, quick success, and a better life often leads to entrapment in the cycle of drugs and eventual incarceration. Instead of becoming contributing members of society they add to the recurring social problem.

The twin burdens of substances abuse and poverty, compounded by a discriminatory and ineffective drug war, are shouldered by communities in our inner cities, and their burdens are generating deeper social divisions within our society. Democratic institutions and values we ought to be strengthening, meanwhile, are being corroded.[30]

Medical

Agreement on statistics that describe the drug problem varies among agencies. The National Institute on Drug Abuse (NIDA), a part of the National Institute of Health, has been researching the scientific and medical effects of illegal drugs since 1974. NIDA has catalogued thought-provoking data regarding drug related deaths for a typical year. NIDA reports that tobacco kills approximately 390,000 Americans per year; alcohol kills 80,000; secondhand smoke kills 50,000; cocaine kills 2,200; aspirin kills 2,000; heroin kills 2,000; and marijuana kills 0.[31] In 1999, NIDA found a total of 4,500 deaths in the United States from direct use of all drugs categorized as illegal, about one-forth the number of traffic deaths attributed to alcohol use and one percent of those killed by alcohol and tobacco combined.[32] Medical costs related to illicit drug use totals over $20 billion.[33] Included in this figure are costs connected with the problem of shared needles which facilitates the spread of both the HIV virus and various strains of hepatitis.

The Center for Disease Control (CDC) is unable to provide a breakdown by substance of annual deaths attributed to drugs but they concede their data includes both legal and illegal drugs. CDC further states that reliable data are not available from any other source to facilitate such a breakdown.[34] The NIDA disagrees: "Tobacco kills more people each year than all of the people killed by all of the illegal drugs in the last century".[35] If true, this fact would indicate that individual health is not a primary consideration for policy.

Costs

Illegal drugs exact a staggering cost on American society. In 1999, Americans spent $63.2 billion on illegal drugs.[36] The Office of National Drug Control Policy (ONDCP) estimates the economic cost of illegal drug use in the United States was $160.7 billion in 2000.[37] In 1995, drugs accounted for an estimated $110 billion in expenses and lost revenue. The expense of the public health burden is shared across society and tax dollars pay for increased enforcement efforts and incarceration as well as treatment and education programs. NIDA estimates that health-care expenditures due to drug abuse cost Americans nearly 40 billion dollars in 1992.[38]

The proposed fiscal year 2007 budget to fund the WoD is $12.7 billion[39] while the repercussions of enforcing current drug laws for federal, state, and local governments add $48 million to that figure.[40] "Since the enactment of mandatory minimum sentencing for drug users, the Federal Bureau of Prisons budget has increased by 1,954%. Its budget jumped from $220 million in 1986 to more than $4.3 billion in 2001."[41] In 2005, over 1.8 million people were arrested for drug law violations and over 80% of those arrests were possession offenses. Fewer than 20% were arrested for manufacture or sale of drugs.[42] According to ONDCP it costs the federal government approximately $3 billion per year to incarcerate drug offenders.[43] The American Corrections Association estimates that state governments spend over $6 billion[44] for the same purpose - the combined figure exceeds $9 billion and the United States now has the highest incarceration rate of all industrialized countries, with 57% of the federal prison population serving time for drug offenses.[45] The indirect costs in terms of impact on families, lost productivity, lost tax revenue, and unrealized potential is difficult to assess. However, "[t]his breakdown reveals that a large part of the price society pays for drug use arises not from the effects of the drugs themselves, but from the cost of enforcing the laws that prohibit them."[46]

One must question if the current strategy is economically viable given the inevitability of higher budget priorities and constrained resources. Milton Friedman made the case against the WoD by describing the problem as:

> ...failing to recognize that the very measures you favor are the major sources of the evils you deplore. Of course the problem is demand, but it is not only demand, it is demand that must operate through repressed and illegal channels. Illegality creates obscene profits that finance the murderous tactics of the drug lords; illegality leads to the corruption of law enforcement officials; illegality monopolized the efforts of honest law forces so that they are starved for resources to fight the simpler crimes of robbery, theft and assault. Drugs are a tragedy for addicts. But criminalizing their use converts that tragedy into a disaster for society, for users and non-users alike. [47]

The Linkage to Terrorist Organizations

US officials and government agencies have consistently proclaimed direct links between the illegal drug trade and terrorism. Indeed, the drug trade rewards the most ruthless, and terrorists have a distinct advantage in this environment. Former House Speaker Dennis Hastert pointed out the financial support that drugs provide. "Narco-terrorists in South America earn a staggering $600 million per year from the illegal drug trade."[48] Hastert also stated that "the illegal drug trade is the financial engine that fuels many terrorist organizations in the world including Osama bin Laden."[49] The Office of Drug Control Policy states that "12 of the 28 terror organizations identified by the State Department in October of 2001, traffic in drugs."[50] The impacts of these organizations are felt regionally. "In Brazil, most of the drug trafficking gangs have direct ties to Colombia's Revolutionary Armed Forces (FARC) guerrillas..."[51]

Not only is it widely accepted that drug traffickers and terrorists are partnered, it is also clear that terrorists such as the FARC are operating as drug traffickers themselves, shifting their objective from political control to the monetary rewards that drugs provide. Terrorists and terrorist groups fight for control of the drug trade because it funds their activities and facilitates their ability to control governments and geographic areas. The FARC has "waged a 40-year insurgency against the Colombian government and has morphed into Colombia's most powerful drug cartel."[52] Given the power, control, regional influence, and money that they gain from drug trafficking, the FARC has little incentive to pursue their initial objective of over-throwing the Colombian government.

Through drug smuggling, terrorists learn to exploit existing seams in the US security apparatus. Further, they learn how to manipulate people and procedures, and how to deceive or bypass monitoring systems and security mechanisms. This practiced range of capabilities enables more reliable future exploitation for purposes other than drug smuggling. The threat this condition poses may prove to be the most critical and difficult challenge in US history. The defeat of those who undeniably threaten the safety and security of America and American interests is the constitutional responsibility of government. The drug trade must be eliminated as a pillar of support for terrorists.

Undermining Legitimate Governments

The value of any interest is proportional to the measure of effort levied to achieve it. The fact that the drug trade morphs so readily to any escalation of initiatives aimed at curtailing it is evidence of the high interest attributed to it. Individuals, cartels, gangs, organized crime, and terrorist groups have successfully reaped staggering profits regardless of the extent of efforts to thwart their success. In some regions, the cartels have become so powerful that they overshadow, mute, or directly control the legitimate governments and promote instability at will.

Related to narco-terrorism, and perhaps the largest scope peripheral effect, is the way the drug trade infects legitimate governments and creates an environment toxic to their survival. In fact, the trend toward democracy that swept across Latin America over the last several decades appears to be teetering. Venezuela, Bolivia, Ecuador, Brazil, Peru, Nicaragua, Colombia, Panama, and Mexico have governance issues and corruption problems that stem directly from the drug trade and these conditions threaten regional stability. The environment fosters safe havens for terrorists, whose presence further degrades the conditions necessary for a stable government.

Until now, experts have maintained that democracy is flourishing in the new global environment. New research, however, shows that economic globalization, while in some ways promoting democracy, also hinders the consolidation of an accountable government in many countries. Indeed, criminal, financial, scientific, social, and political factors are combining to threaten the international political environment.[53] Many of these factors have direct ties to the illicit drug trade.

<u>Analysis</u>

Tremendous efforts have been made by the international community, billions have been spent by the United States, and large drug cartels have been disassembled, yet drugs still transit freely across US borders and into communities all over the globe. Drug traffickers continue to reap steady profit, while US strategy expends resources with no long-term impact on the drug trade - exacting further and even greater secondary effects. The violence, corruption, and social ills that flourish amidst the profits of the illicit trade make it ever more difficult to counter. "Despite eight decades of international action by the League of Nations and the United Nations ... the problems associated with all aspects of the drug phenomenon ... have increased" not decreased. The link between supply and demand, the drug trade, has proven difficult to fracture.[54] Although there is considerable evidence identifying US policy as failed, the perception of failure is mitigated by the message of stakeholders.

The 1996 National Drug Control Strategy included the following statements:

- "Between 1975 and the early 1990's, the number of new heroin users dropped by 25%."

- "The number of new cocaine users plummeted from a million and a half in 1980 to about half a million in 1992. Overall, cocaine use has fallen 30% in the last three years alone." [55]

Although interesting, these statements pertain to "new" users and thus to a lessened increase in heroin and cocaine use, not to an overall trend of decreased use. It also fails to account for the dramatic increase in the use of other drugs such as methamphetamine.

Clearly, statistics can be misleading, and for some, managing public perception takes priority over truthfulness regarding the effects of strategy. Consider this 1999 White House press release:

> A long term commitment to fight drugs. Year in and year out, the Clinton-Gore Administration has proposed the largest anti-drug budgets ever, helping to increase federal counter-drug spending by nearly 40% between FY93 and FY99. Our sustained effort is having an impact: overall drug use is half the level it was at its peak in the 1970's; drug-related murders are down by 40% since 1992; the

first-ever paid anti-drug media campaign has been launched nationwide; and youth drug use is on the decline for the second year in a row. The 1999 National Drug Control Strategy builds on this progress and takes the next step to reduce drug use and availability across the board. [56]

The "largest anti-drug budgets ever" indicate an increased level of effort to achieve what has not yet come to fruition – enduring strategic success. The level of peak drug use in the 1970's is not quantified nor is the preponderance of use tied to a specific drug, some of which have affects magnitudes more detrimental than others. Thus it is difficult to assess the true impact of the use. We are merely informed that "use is half the level it was in the 1970's." This statistic spanned a period of three decades, but subsequent information on "youth drug use" has a much shorter assessment period – only two years.

Success in interdiction, breaking cartels, and making key arrests is muted by the undeniable continuation of the problem. Both leadership and policy are at risk for loss of credibility and ultimately loss of public support. Political reliance on the policy message as a domestic political tool is the primary cause. Eventually, the public will not be able to reconcile the purported "success" of the WoD when faced with the obvious continuation of the drug problem itself.

Policy is as much a message as it is a collective of national objectives. Recent history has given rise to the dilution of policy goals without any substantive change in policy. We have witnessed the evolution of policy goals from "a drug free America" to the more recent percentages of "reduction in use" as evidenced by the evolution of policy goals:

- Executive Order 12564 of 1986 called for all federal employees to be drug free as a condition of employment, and for each federal agency to develop a "drug-free workplace" program.
- The Anti-Drug Abuse Act of 1988 established the Reagan policy goal to create a "drug-free America" by 1995, which included the establishment of the Office of National Drug Control Policy.[57]
- The 2004 National Drug Control Strategy Goals identified both "a 10% reduction in current use of illegal drugs by 8th, 10th, and 12th graders" and "a 10% reduction in use of illegal drugs by adults age 18 and over". The 5 year goal increased those reduction goals to 25%.[58]

The 2006 strategy claims success. It states that the 2004 policy goal of "reducing youth drug use by 10 percent in two years" was not only achieved, but that the "goal has been met and exceeded."[59] A 10% reduction in use is undeniably more achievable than a "drug free America", but it fails to address 90% of the problem that had been part of the earlier policy goal.

12

Closer scrutiny, however, reveals that the reduction statistic cited was based on a higher 2001 benchmark and not on the 2004 level. Further, both reductions and surges in drug use occur in cycles, thus, a snapshot in time is neither indicative of a trend nor predictive, and should not be hailed as a sign of overall success. It is of little wonder that statistics and datum can leave an audience with the wrong impression. Information is easily manipulated to manage perceptions.

What is clear is that policy goals have been modified to make them achievable while the strategy to achieve that policy has remained unchanged despite the lack of enduring results. In short, goals changed in order to make policy appear more successful, thus justifying and promoting a continuation of policy. But the obligation of government is greater than continuity of effort – government must ensure that national policy effort is well conceived and that the relationship between policy and strategy is harmonious.

Political Paradox

Johnny Holloway of the American University School of International Service when addressing the Annual Meeting of the International Studies Association explained that because of closed minds, proponents of the status quo of the WoD have the capacity to:

> …operate on a separate plane of existence, a morally righteous high ground, that allows these practitioners not only to deny the validity of the facts and evidence that outline the flaws in their mantra but also to assault and intimidate any bearers of contrary evidence by linking them with crime, sexual deviance, [and] questioning their patriotism…to such an extent that implementing or discussing fundamental change is effectively precluded.[60]

Holloway's evaluation is exacting while difficult to fathom. Polarization of the interest groups prevents an honest, factual, scientific approach. A rational analysis of facts and trends would go far in advancing public interest and understanding – but stakeholders seem committed to achieving personal objectives instead of better managing the problem. The benefit of nearly a century of documented hindsight (from the Harrison Act, Prohibition and 30 years of statistics on the WoD) is available as a guide, but political fear has policy makers mired in the current strategy.

An iterative cycle seems to have developed - failure followed by an escalation of effort. While policy demands the expenditure of resources and politicians foster the public perception of a "no holds barred" and "get tough" approach to the drug problem, the drug trade seems to benefit. The policy message has resonated with the American public despite the fact that it has not proven effective in either resolving or managing the drug problem. Perceptions and attitudes are changing, however. Many websites and organizations have begun to shed light on

13

the drug problem and the effects of the current counter-drug strategy. As one would expect, in an impatient society, political rhetoric is a reality that can carry public will only a finite distance.

Supply and Demand

> The federal anti-drug initiative has two major elements: (1) reduction of demand and (2) reduction of supply. Reduction of demand is sought through education to prevent dependence, through treatment to cure addiction and through measures to increase prices and risk of apprehension at the consumer level. Reduction of supply, which currently accounts for about 64.5% of the federal anti-drug control budget, is sought by programs aimed at destabilizing the operations of illicit drug cartels at all levels and severing their links to political power, and by seizing their products, businesses, and financial assets.[61]

Drugs have become a commodity. The illicit drug trade is best viewed as an illegal business and not as a "war" with political objectives. There is no better example of the law of supply and demand than the illicit drug trade. This immutable economic law, that supply will find a means to meet demand, and that price and profit will fluctuate proportionally, has proved more powerful than all the elements of US power combined. Indeed, despite ardent US efforts to prevent illicit imports, the supply of illegal drugs has proven unstoppable. A study conducted by the United Nations revealed enormous profit margins on illegal drugs sold in the United States. "In 2001, a kilogram of heroin in Pakistan sold for an average of $610 [while] in the United States heroin cost an average of $25,000 per kilogram."[62] With incentive levels this high, producers, smugglers, or pushers who are arrested and imprisoned are quickly replaced by others eager to assume the same risks.[63]

Profit Paradox

The United States maintains weighted efforts aimed at the reduction of external supply coming into the country. Despite some successful interdiction efforts, street prices for drugs are lower in many instances. "Over the past decade, inflation-adjusted prices in Western Europe fell by 45% for cocaine and 60% for heroin...comparative falls in the United States were about 50% for cocaine and 70% for heroin."[64] Supply capability continues to meet and exceed demand despite these weighted efforts. What should be clear messages to US policy makers is that a focus on external supply restriction is wrong-headed. As long as the tremendous profit potential endures, there will be individuals willing to assume risk to achieve those disproportionate gains.

Because the drug war raises profits as it raises prices, the stick of law enforcement that is intended to discourage suppliers on the black market simultaneously creates a carrot of enormous profits – which encourages suppliers. As they pursue high profits, they keep the supply of drugs up and that prevents prices from rising too high which, in turn, undermines the aim of policy. As Steven Wisotsky, author of "Beyond the War on Drugs: Overcoming a Failed Public Policy" explains, "If the cocaine industry commissioned a consultant to design a mechanism to ensure its profitability, it would not have done better than the War on Drugs: just enough pressure to inflate prices, but not enough to keep its product from the market."[65] The more a supply source is constricted the greater the incentive for alternative sources to emerge; as one might expect, the immutable law of supply and demand makes any success short-lived.

This well-known "profit paradox" allows cartels and drug lords to spend more to maintain the illicit trade than most governments can budget to prevent it. Every strategy developed to deter or prevent the smuggling of illegal drugs into the United States is met with a counter-strategy. For example: The eradication of the large drug cartels of the 1980's resulted in the formation of smaller entities, a phenomenon known as the "hydra-effect."[66] These smaller groups are proving even more difficult to locate, infiltrate, and prosecute; boats are being manufactured with the capability of carrying up to two tons of cocaine at higher speeds; "black cocaine" is being created using a new chemical process that makes it impossible for drug sniffing dogs to find.[67]

Blockades have never proven effective on a continental power with large coastlines. In fact, it is largely through this failed British strategy that the Colonies won independence. A strategy of supply denial is in effect, a self-imposed blockade. Consider the following: the United States has approximately 20,000 kilometers of shoreline, 300 ports of entry and more than 7,500 miles of border with Mexico and Canada, and must contend with competing national priorities and a fixed budget with which to wage the WoD. Add to this the fact that "…thirteen truck loads of cocaine are enough to satisfy US demand for one year." [68] How, with obstacles such as these, can the United States expect to achieve success by relying primarily on a strategy of supply denial?

Demand

Demand for drugs within a society is a reflection of the values of that society. Thus, the values and involvement of society are key factors in facilitating the drug problem, just as they are essential components in mitigating it. Demand is the core problem as well as the condition that enables the drug trade. Supply manifests to satisfy what demand dictates and profit facilitates.

The sad truth is that there will always be drug users among us. Studies indicate that individuals born with fewer D2 receptors on their brains are predisposed to drug addiction.

These receptors are the mechanism through which dopamine acts to stimulate pleasurable feelings. Since drug use stimulates dopamine outflow at elevated levels the drive to preserve these elevated levels is a powerful force that often leads to addiction.[69] A case in point is methamphetamine. One of the most addictive of all drugs, methamphetamine is also one of the most damaging to the human brain. It can be produced at home using readily available over the counter drugs and chemicals available at any hardware store - its use is near epidemic.[70]

Curiosity, experimentation, recreational use, and physical predisposition will cause some to fall victim to the seduction of drugs. Thus, even if the WoD were 100% successful in eliminating external supply, some users would seek alternative means to achieve an altered state of mind through domestic manufacture or use of readily available products (huffing, ingesting poisonous mushrooms, etc..).

Between 1989 and 1998, Americans spent somewhere between $39 and $77 billion on cocaine and $10 to $22 billion on heroin, annually.[71] Despite the fact that federal government spending on the WoD increased from $1.65 billion in 1982 to $18.5 billion in 2002, more than half of high school students in the United States reported trying an illegal drug before they graduated, and during every year from 1975 to 1999, 82% of all high school seniors surveyed indicated that they could find marijuana fairly to very easily.[72] On the surface the statistics seem to indicate that supply restriction was not effective during this period; however, it also indicates that the criminality of drug use is not recognized by this demographic group; thus lack of regard for the rule of law, a value critical to democracy, appears to be a peripheral effect within US society.

Continuity of drug education is perhaps the best approach for the long term. Public education programs and awareness efforts have long been used to influence public opinion and to dissuade new users; however, many of those efforts are being curtailed before they can take effect. "Abstinence education programs for youth have proven effective in reducing early sexual activity", a fact that indicates behaviors can be influenced through education without punitive enforcement measures.[73] According to the Center for Disease Control, the percentage of sexually active teens has dropped from 54% in the early 1990's to only 46% today. This downward trend coincides with the increased educational effort aimed at the problem.[74]The National Youth Anti-Drug Media Campaign received its first Congressional appropriation in 1998 for $195 Million. The legislation required media companies to match government funds through the donation of equivalent advertising toward the anti-drug effort. In 2000 a freelance investigative reporter made claims that the government was exercising too much control over this anti-drug advertising. Follow-on investigation indicated that the matching donations were not being properly managed. The controversy resulted in Congressional oversight and a change in appropriations language in 2001 to better manage control – but Congress subsequently demonstrated reluctance and has reduced funding for the media campaign every year since 2001.[75]

In 2002, NIDA released a report based on household surveys that found the youth media campaign had little effect on drug use by young Americans between 2000 and 2001. It stated:

> There is little evidence of direct favorable Campaign effects on youth. There is no statistically significant decline in marijuana use to date, and some evidence for an increase in use from 2000 to 2001. Nor are there improvements in beliefs and attitudes about marijuana use between 2000 and the first half of 2002. Contrarily, there are some unfavorable trends in youth anti-marijuana beliefs. Also there is no tendency for those reporting more exposure to Campaign messages to hold more desirable beliefs.[76]

The problem with the report and its assumption is it is based upon a one year period – a snapshot in time. It takes time for education to have its effect. When first and second graders learn about the adverse effects of drugs over the course of elementary school – it is reasonable to assume there will be a positive affect. It is not equally reasonable to assume that the opinions or behaviors of older students will be swayed after a one year media campaign.

Drug education efforts must start early and be reinforced regularly over a prolonged period of time in order to develop meaningful data trends. "If boys and girls grow to maturity without using illegal drugs, alcohol, or tobacco, they are likely to remain drug free for the rest of their lives. Rarely does a person begin drug abuse after the age of twenty."[77] Education is a long term investment with long term dividends as the objective – a short-term assessment will not reveal progress toward that objective. It takes time for the young, grade school audience to reach high school age where the effect of education and prevention can be reflected. Politicians appear too easily influenced by scrutiny and criticism from the media.

Policy Paradox

US drug policy and strategy currently maintain a strong external focus despite the detrimental effects levied on other US policy objectives. The net result is a kind of policy fratricide. Together, the policy and strategy adversely affect perceptions of the United States abroad, impair future critical partnerships, and dissuade governments from assisting the United States, often turning them instead toward US peer competitors. An external focus facilitates a domestic lack of responsibility and accountability, and enables a sense of victimization through existential threats: gangs, organized crime, cartels, violence, corruption, rogue states, and narco-terrorism. It detracts attention from the internal factors more responsible for the domestic drug problem, encouraging the continuation of both a detrimental policy and its failed strategy.

In addition to an external focus, strategy emphasizes tactical operations that target lower-level actors to limit supply and deter use. Colombian officials "seized a record amount of coca products in 1998 - almost 57 metric tons - and also destroyed 185 cocaine laboratories... [However] there has not been a net reduction in processing or exporting refined cocaine from Colombia or in cocaine availability within the United States."[78] "Despite 2 years of extensive herbicide spraying [source country eradication], estimates show there has not been any net reduction in [Colombian] coca cultivation - net coca cultivation actually increased 50 percent."[79] US incarceration rates and prison budgets have dramatically increased, yet "if one compares 1996 to 1984, the crime index is 13 points higher. This dramatic increase occurred during an era of mandatory minimum sentencing and 'three strikes you're out'."[80] There are many such examples that clearly demonstrate the failure of strategy.

Action taken in accordance with current strategy yields little beneficial strategic effect and spawns paralyzing peripheral impacts that actually benefit the drug trade and adversely impact both society and US national security strategy. Yet drug strategy continues to reflect the expectations inherent to the "American way of war": resources are piled high and violent efforts are intensified toward the pursuit of a decisive victory.[81] The strategy is expensive, ineffective and yields detrimental effects, yet political support to effect a change in either policy or strategy is mute.

Drug policy currently has the United States mired in a destructive policy paradox. Political leadership rigidly adheres to traditional policy despite its failure and regardless of its harmful effects upon US interests. In a sense policy is digging its own grave. The greater the intensity with which the WoD is waged, the more rapidly resources and public confidence in its success will be eroded. The United States is by nature an impatient society. It is only a matter of time before cost intensive measures are curtailed and resources are shifted to other priorities. With forethought and action, however, a resurgence of drug use can be prevented.

An Alternative Strategy

A revised US counter-drug strategy requires the development of a national drug policy that deals effectively with the international drug trade and provides a comprehensive and beneficial approach to overarching policy. Policy must be devoid of detrimental impacts, address the drug problem internal to the United States, and promote international cooperation. It must be feasible, suitable, sustainable, and in the end, acceptable to the American public.

Ultimately, the strategy must achieve the buy-in required to implement and maintain the effort. The following steps are proposed:

- Maintain an economy of force effort and gradually phase in the revised strategy.
- Break the current paradigm. Advertise the detrimental effects of the current strategy and the benefits of the revised approach.
- Educate the public. Provide factual information. The intent of this long term initiative is to reduce demand through an enhanced understanding of the effects of drugs – not to merely foster a negative public perception of drug use. Selective focus. Shift focus from lower-level actors and activities that have little strategic impact to higher-level actors and businesses that benefit from the drug trade.
- Restructure penalization. Revise sentencing guidelines for users and low-level actors that are resource intensive and have no strategic effect on the drug trade.
- Reassess strategic effects. Policy and strategy must continually be adjusted. Strategy must evolve with society and with global conditions in order to maintain public support and remain effective.

Economy of Force

An economy of force effort can be waged to maintain pressure on the trade while the long-term strategy is gradually phased into place. This approach is intended to prevent escalation and to maintain continuity while the American public becomes better informed and elements of the revised strategy are implemented. The US government must gradually shift intense efforts away from the many aspects of the drug trade and concentrate resources on the critical constructs that support the business model and on the education of future generations. Interdiction and supply efforts cannot be halted abruptly, but as demand is reduced through education, the level of effort devoted to interdiction can be curtailed.

Break the Paradigm

Politicians will not change their stripes. The rhetoric, self-interest, and protection of interests will continue, but accurate information and glaring truth can levy tremendous pressure and potentially a public mandate for change. To break the American paradigm of what the WoD should look like, the Administration must find the right messengers, use the right communication vehicles, and send the right message consistently. The failure of Prohibition's "noble experiment" should be a guide. Political fear and rhetoric must be overcome in favor of unbiased facts, truthful statistics, and meaningful trends. Americans must know and understand the effects that drugs have on individuals, America, and global society and they must be informed regarding the costs and adverse effects of the current US strategy.

A cost-benefit analysis presented clearly and through a wide range of accepted forums - a Presidential Address to the nation, member of Congress, media pundits, and Public Service Announcements, and a national media campaign - could provide the American people basic economic facts and educate them on the second and third order effects of the drug trade. In light of that information, it would be reasonable to assume that the public, and subsequently their representatives in state legislatures and the Congress, would be open to reconsider how we might more prudently craft an anti-drug policy and execute an anti-drug strategy.

Education

The core of the drug problem, demand, lies within the bounds of American society to influence. Through reduction of demand in the world's wealthiest country there will necessarily be global impact on supply and profit. In addition to global strategic effect, efforts directed at domestic demand require no international agreement, host nation support, or military action abroad. These efforts include little risk when compared to the more aggressive and invasive methodologies of enforcement and interdiction. Risk of being drawn into an insurgency, civil conflict, or a prolonged war with narco-terrorists would be mitigated. Even resource requirements should remain relatively static once education programs are established.

It is essential for the American public to understand the peripheral effects of the drug trade; how the poor are manipulated, the vulnerable are abused, children are victimized and developing nations are destroyed while terrorists and criminals become wealthy. The new strategy would wage the anti-drug effort by reducing demand through dramatically enhanced programs in the vane of the "D.A.R.E.," "Just Say No," and "Scared Straight" programs – but new programs would be aimed at educating the young with a long term perspective rather than a short-term focus on deterring behavior directly. In addition, a media and role model campaign would be reinitiated to target reduction of drug use through social pressure.

During the war years of 1941-45, the US government tapped Hollywood to participate in the making of newsreels and themed movies to uplift the troops and the American people. In more recent history, "Public Service Announcements" by popular TV and movie stars have continued that WWII tradition in attempts to reduce the domestic demand for drugs.

A massive public awareness effort tied to public school education that focuses on school age children is essential. Policy makers must have the courage to stand-up to critics and those who oppose a public education approach. Information and education is the center of gravity for a democracy, and ultimately, the people will decide what values their society reflects and what laws govern their society. If the 64.5% budget effort extended to fight supply[82] were instead shifted to better manage demand, one would see lasting reductions in demand as well as subsequent decreases in supply. Demand remains within the national ability to constantly shape and influence and must be the focal point of the national effort. The current drug education effort is anemic and requires a significant transfusion of funding.

Selective Focus

The business aspects of the drug trade involve raw material acquisition, cultivation, production and processing efforts, transportation and distribution operations, marketing, sales, and revenue operations (collection, money laundering, and distribution). With the best of intentions, a government can easily find itself overextended trying to fight a war on every front. An element of the policy paradox exists within these actions as they serve to deplete resources and eventually exhaust public will. The policy is tantamount to fighting everywhere and winning nowhere.

Efforts to continue the drug trade will be proportional to the profit potential, but the ability to continue the trade will ultimately be dictated by profit realized. Minimal profit will result in a minimal drug trade. Profit is the ultimate goal of the trafficker and, as the center of gravity for the industry, it must be targeted. The core of a business-based strategy must be to deny the realization of profits and to aggressively pursue the prosecution of key actors and facilitators. Corrupt officials who facilitate the trade and key actors who coordinate and benefit from it must be ferreted out and punished severely. Those who would replace them must be convinced that there is no future in the drug trade.

An international consensus to combat money laundering is essential in this global financial age – a strong alliance of economic enforcement and cooperation must be formed. Profit must be targeted and seized by the alliance; not realized by the illicit business operators. This alliance would unify partner countries toward a common goal and a common good, and isolate those who continue to facilitate the drug trade. This approach would mitigate the view of the United States as a hegemon that intervenes in the affairs of sovereign nations, not to help them, but to achieve US interests. It also creates a buffer zone between the United States and non-compliant source countries. This would provide the opportunity for international diplomacy and economic elements of power to have considerable impact and decrease the likelihood of the United States being drawn into a civil war or conflict with narco-terrorists. Support can be provided to allied source countries from the alliance account – built through contributions, seized drug profits, and confiscated assets.

Restructured Penalization

Clearly, we cannot control drug use by cutting off the external supply of drugs, but we can better manage internal demand by persuading a change in behavior vice attempting to mandate it. Strict enforcement efforts and mandatory sentences for users and low level operators have proven a cost intensive and ineffective way to combat the drug trade. Lost productivity, overcrowded prisons, over-burdened judicial systems and under-manned law enforcement have demonstrated the inefficiency and ineffectiveness of this approach. Restructured penalization calls for the significant overhaul of sentencing guidelines for the possession and use of certain drugs. No longer would there be jail time but, rather fines and community service requirements. The objective is three fold:

- To reduce the cost of enforcement by diminishing court case loads and decreasing inmate population by more than one half;[83]
- To focus effort and resources to a greater strategic effect; and
- To provide services to communities and incentive for users not to re-offend.

It is acknowledged that a break from the punitive paradigm will neither be clean nor complete. The effort to restructure penalization will meet with especially strong resistance and will not be adopted readily. Some will predict an increase in drug use and others will foster that fear as an obstruction to change. Billions of dollars are tied to enforcement efforts and many programs and jobs are directly impacted. No agency or organization tied to this funding will voluntarily act to divest itself of resources and most will resist any initiative that would curtail funding.

Legalization is not recommended. History has shown that legalization increases drug use.[84] Decriminalization, however, is a way to restructure penalization and better focus anti-drug efforts. This effort may meet with significant resistance from citizens' groups and special interest organizations that are emotionally vested in the WoD and have supported use of the military as the primary line of defense against international drug trafficking. Politicians will be especially wary of taking any position that would cause them to appear soft on drugs or crime – especially if any associated cost reductions affect voters in their district.

A daunting task confronts agents for change since part of the "right messenger" requirement must include these groups and the "right message" requires that they reach consensus and pursue the revised strategy with a sense of unity and resolve. It is unlikely that legislators or an administration will pursue decriminalization unless public pressure results in a mandate for change, and that mandate is unlikely to occur unless politicians have the courage to campaign for it – another element of the current political paradox.

Conclusion

The United States has expended huge resources to achieve particular policy goals, but even short-term successes have merely served to bolster on-going efforts while enhancing the power, capability, potential and profits of drug traffickers. Worse, the peripheral impacts tied to the drug trade by nature undermine legitimate governments, respect for law, and regional stability. The state of corruption, violence, coercion and chaos that grow from the drug trade serve to preclude legitimate governments from functioning effectively. These impacts set the stage for a much more damaging range of scenarios that adversely affect US security and national interests.

The WoD is a classic strategy-policy mismatch that creates one paradox after another. The political reality is a strategy of self-defeat. As it exists today, the WoD is neither suitable nor sustainable and lacks vision given present circumstances and the threat outlook. The policy has become a political tool rather than an achievable national objective. The strategy, although culturally acceptable, is both a tactical and a strategic failure. The status quo policy is not viable if the actual objective is to curtail the drug trade.

Policy must be adjusted, or strategy crafted that better considers and appreciates the many peripheral impacts of strategy as well as the primary objectives of policy. Political will to modify policy is weak, but sound policy cannot demand of strategy what strategy cannot achieve. If the Administration will not reassess current strategy, then Congress must. Oversight authority should be enacted to reassess the WoD and facilitate the shift in policy that is needed to correct ineffective focus and alleviate the associated burdens that adversely affect society. We must transition to an economic strategy that targets not the supply but the immense profitability of the illegal drug business, and use the conserved resources to achieve leveraged benefits that enhance our society and its national security posture. Through education, we can successfully wage an effective long-term and cost effective anti-drug strategy, but we must break our short-term paradigm. We must develop strategic patience. In so doing, we can better achieve policy goals and focus resources on future threats to US national security.

The United States must shift its paradigm – the effort to counter illicit drugs is not a war to be won or lost, but a problem better managed than solved.

Endnotes

[1] The White House, "The Purposes and Nature of Strategy," in *The National Drug Control Strategy: 1997* (Washington, D.C.: The White House, 1997); available from http://www.ncjrs.gov/htm/chapter1.htm#overview; Internet; accessed 18 February 2007.

[2] Ludwig von Mises, *Human Action: A Treatise on Economic:* (Chicago: Regency Publishing, 1966), 733.

[3] The White House, *The National Drug Control Strategy 2000 Annual Report* (Washington, D.C.: The White House, 2000), 2-3; available from http://www.ncjrs.gov/ondcppubs/publications/policy/ndcs00/strategy2000.pdf; Internet; accessed; 18 February 2007. Hereafter cited as *The National Drug Control Strategy 2000 Annual Report.*

[4] G.L. Henderson, "Designer Drugs: Past History and Future Prospects," *Journal of Foreign Sciences*, 33 (March 1988): 569-575; quoted in Mandy Bentham, *The Politics of Drug Control* (New York: Macmillan/St. Martin's Press, 1998), 60.

[5] B.L. Bentson and D.W. Rasmussen, "Predatory Public Finance and the Origins of War on Drugs," *The Independent Review* 1 (Fall 1996): 163-189.

[6] Ronald Chepesiuk, *The War on Drugs: An International Encyclopedia* (Santa Barbara, CA: ABC-CLIO, 1999), xxii-iii.

[7] Ibid., xxiii.

[8] Ibid., xxiv.

[9] Ibid., xxviii

[10] Ibid., 261.

[11] Ibid., xxxii.

[12] Steven L. Taylor, "When Wars Collide: The War on Drugs and the Global War on Terror," *Strategic Insights* 4 (June 2005): 1.

[13] National Criminal Justice Reference Service, "Drug Control Strategy: An Overview," *The Purposes and Nature of Strategy,* 4; available from www.ncjrs.gov/htm/chapter1.htm; Internet; accessed 18 February 2007.

[14] The White House, "The Purposes and Nature of Strategy," in *The National Drug Control Strategy:* 1997 (Washington, D.C.: The White House, 1997); available from http://www.ncjrs.gov/htm/chapter1.htm#overview; Internet; accessed 18 February 2007.

[15] Ibid.

[16] Mark Thornton, *Alcohol Prohibition Was a Failure* (Washington, D.C.: CATO Institute, 17 July 1991); *available* from http://www.cato.org/pub_display.php?pub_id=1017&full=1; Internet; accessed 05 November 2006.

[17] Douglas A. McVay, "Drug War Facts: Crime," September 2006; available from http://www.drugwarfacts.org/crime.txt; Internet; accessed 4 February 2007.

[18] Isabel Vincent, "Where the Drug Lords Are King," *Maclean's 120* (29 January 2007): 24.

[19] "The Americas: The Tough Get Going: Crime in Mexico," *The Economist* 382 (27 January 2007): 33. Hereafter cited as "The Tough Get Going."

[20] *Richard Cowan Homepage* (2001); available from www.richardcowan.org; Internet; accessed 10 November 2006.

[21] "The Americas: The Tough Get Going," 33.

[22] Vincent, 24.

[23] Trade and Environment Database (TED), *Case Studies: Columbia Coca Trade* (Washington, D.C.: American University, 1997); available from http://www.drugwarfacts.org/environm.txt; Internet; accessed 4 February 2007.

[24] Douglas A. McVay, "Drug War Facts: Corruption," September 2006; available from http://www.drugwarfacts.org/corrupt.txt; Internet; accessed 4 February 2007.

[25] General Accounting Office, Report to the Honorable Charles B. Rangel, House of Representatives, *Law Enforcement: Information on Drug-Related Police Corruption* (Washington, D.C.: U.S. Government Printing Office, May 1998), 35; available from http://www.drugwarfacts.org/corrupt.txt; Internet; accessed 5 November 2006.

[26] David C. Jordan, "Same Drugs, Same Dangers," *The Washington Post*, 25 December 1999 [database on-line]; available from ProQuest; accessed 21 March 2007.

[27] J. M. Hagedom, *The Business of Drug Dealing in Milwaukee* (Milwaukee: Wisconsin Policy Research Institute, 1998), 1.

[28] E. Blumenson and E.S. Nilsen, "How to Construct an Underclass, or How the War on Drugs Became a War on Education," *The Journal of Gender, Race and Justice* 6 (May 2002).

[29] Mark Eddy, *War on Drugs: Legislation in the 108th Congress and Related Developments* (Washington, D.C.: Library of Congress, Congressional Research Service, 3 October 2004), 10.

[30] Eva Bertram et al., *Drug War Politics: The Price of Denial* (Berkeley: University of California Press, 1996), 53.

[31] *Schaffer Library of Drug Policy*; available from http://www.druglibrary.org/schaffer/library/basicfax3.htm; Internet; accessed 23 March 2007.

[32] "Costs to Society," linked from "Archived NIDA Research Monographs," *National Institute on Drug Abuse Homepage,* 2004; available from www.nida.nih.gov; Internet; accessed 10 November 2006.

[33] "Drug War Facts: Economics," linked from *Common Sense for Drug Policy,* 2004, 9; available from www.drugwarfacts.org; Internet; accessed 10 November 2006.

[34] Raphael F. Perl, *International Drug Trade and U.S. Foreign Policy* (Washington, D.C.: Library of Congress, Congressional Research Service, 6 November 2006), 2.

[35] *Schaffer Library of Drug Policy.*

[36] *The* National *Drug Control Strategy 2000 Annual Report*, 28.

[37] Eddy, 2.

[38] National Institute on Drug Abuse, "Health Costs" table, *NIDA Notes*, Vol. 13, no 4; available from http://www.drugabuse.gov/NIDA_Notes/NNVol13N4/Abusecosts.html; Internet; accessed 25 March 2007.

[39] The White House, *National Drug Control Strategy: FY 2007 Budget Summary* (Washington, D.C.: The White House, 2006), 3; available from http://www.whitehousedrugpolicy.gov/publications/policy/07budget/budget07.pdf; Internet; accessed 10 November 2006.

[40] Drug Sense, "Drug War Clock," (28 March 2004); available from www.drugsense.org; Internet; accessed 10 November 2006.

[41] U.S. Department of Justice, *Sourcebook of Criminal Justice Statistics 1996* (Washington, D.C.: U.S. Department of Justice, Bureau of Justice Statistics, 1997), 20; and Executive Office of the President, *Budget of the United States Government, FY 2002* (Washington, D.C.: U.S. Government Printing Office, 2001), 134; available from http://www.drugwarfacts.org/prison.txt; Internet; accessed 10 November 2006.

[42] "Crime," linked from *Drug War Facts*; available from http://www.drugwarfacts.org/crime.htm; Internet; accessed 23 March 2007.

[43] "Drug Offenders in the Corrections System – Prisons, Jails and Probation," linked from *Drug War Facts*; available from http://www.drugwarfacts.org/prison.htm; Internet; accessed 23 March 2007.

[44] Ibid.

[45] Eddy, 2.

[46] Ibid.

[47] Bertram, et al., 182.

[48] Denis Hastert, "Floor Speech, U.S. House of Representatives," *Congressional Record* 148 (4 February 2002).

[49] Malia Rulon, "Hastert Forms Task Force on Drugs," 21 September 2001 [database on-line]; available from LexisNexis; accessed 23 March 2007.

[50] *Drugs and Terror: Understanding the Link and the Impact on America*; available from http://web.archive.org/web/20041027204854/www.theantidrug.com/drugs_terror/understanding_impact.asp; Internet; accessed 23 March 2007.

[51] Vincent, 24.

[52] Ibid.

[53] David C. Jordon, *Drug Politics: Dirty Money and Democracies* (Norman: University of Oklahoma Press, 1999), 5.

[54] Mandy Bentham, *The Politics of Drug Control* (New York: Macmillan/St. Martin's Press: 1998), 117.

[55] The White House, "Cause for Guarded Optimism," *National Drug Control Strategy: 1996*; available from www.usinfo.state.gov/journals/itgic/0796/ijge/ejinfo1.html; Internet; accessed 5 December 2006.

[56] The U.S. Department of Health and Human Services, "Vice President Gore Unveils 1999 National Dug Control Strategy," White House Press Release, Office of the Vice President, 8 February 1999; available from www.dhhs.gov/news/press/1999pres/19990208.html; Internet; accessed 6 December 2006.

[57] *The National Drug Control Strategy 2000 Annual Report.*

[58] The White House, *National Drug Control Strategy 2004* (Washington, D.C.: The White House, March 2004), 3; available from http://www.state.gov/documents/organization/30228.pdf; Internet; accessed 18 February 2007.

[59] The White House, *National Drug Control Strategy 2006* (Washington, D.C.: The White House, February 2006), 1; available from http://www.whitehousedrugpolicy.gov/ publications/policy/ndcs06/ndcs06.pdf; Internet; accessed 18 February 2007.

[60] J. Holloway, "The Military Reflex of the Body Politic: Thinking Critically about the United States' War on Drugs," *43rd Annual Meeting of the International Studies Association* (New Orleans: International Studies Association, 2002); available from http://www.isanet.org/ noarchive/holloway.html; Internet; accessed 25 March 2007.

[61] Perl, 5.

[62] United Nations, *Global Illicit Drug Trends: 2003* (New York: United Nations, Office on Drugs and Crime, 2003), 243; available from http://www.unodc.org/pdf/trends2003_www_E.pdf; Internet; accessed 25 March 2007.

[63] Timothy Lynch, *After Prohibition: An Adult Approach to Drug Policies in the 21st Century* (Washington, D.C.: CATO Institute, 2000), 96.

[64] *Global Illicit Drug Trends: 2003,* 86.

[65] Bertram et al., 13.

[66] Jordan, *Drug Politics: Dirty Money and Democracies*, 16.

[67] U.S. General Accounting Office, *Drug Control: Narcotics Threat from Colombia Continues to Grow* (Washington, D.C.: U.S. Government Printing Office, 1999), 4-5.

[68] Douglas A. McVay, "Drug War Facts: Interdiction," February 2004; available from http://www.drugwarfacts.org/interdic.txt; Internet; accessed 4 February 2007.

[69] Robert Mathias, "Pathological Obesity and Drug Addiction Share Common Brain Characteristics," National Institute on Drug Abuse, *NIDA Notes*, Vol. 16, no 4; available from http://www.nida.nih.gov/NIDA_Notes/NNVol16N4/pathological.html; Internet; accessed 24 March 2007; and Genevieve Maul, "Addiction Breakthrough May Lead to New Treatments," University of Cambridge, 1 March 2007; available from http://www.eurekalert. org/ pub_releases/2007-03/uoc-amb022607.php; Internet; accessed 24 March 2007.

[70] Doctor Jack Stump, Chairman, Department of Emergency Medicine Southwest Washington Hospital, telephone interview by author, 7 March 2007. Dr. Stump is a world renowned expert on methamphetamine addiction and is a frequent speaker at medical symposiums. The US Drug Enforcement Agency relies on his expertise and has referenced his work in DEA publications. The FBI regards him as a top authority on methamphetamine use.

[71] The White House, *What American Users Spend on Illegal Drugs 1988-1999* (Washington, D.C.: The White House, Office of National Drug Control Policy, 2000), 5.

[72] Douglas A. McVay, "Drug War Facts: Interdiction."

[73] Robert E. Rector, *The Effectiveness of Abstinence Education Programs in Reducing Sexual Activity Among Youth,* Backgrounder 1533 (Washington D.C.: The Heritage Foundation, 8 April 2002); available from http://www.heritage.org/research/abstinence/BG1533.cfm; Internet; accessed on 15 March 2007.

[74] Wade F. Horn and Jeffrey S. Trimbath, "Another Reason for Abstinence," available from http://www.acf.hhs.gov/programs/fysb/content/news/060518.htm; Internet; accessed 15 March 2007.

[75] Mark Eddy, *War on Drugs: The National Youth Anti-Drug Media Campaign* (Washington, D.C.: Library of Congress, Congressional Research Service, 3 July 2006), 1-5.

[76] Ibid.

[77] The White House, "A Comprehensive Approach," in *The National Drug Control Strategy: 1997* (Washington, D.C.: The White House, 1997); available from http://www.ncjrs.gov/ htm/chapter4.htm; Internet; accessed 18 February 2007.

[78] U.S. General Accounting Office, *Drug Control: Narcotics Threat from Colombia Continues to Grow* (Washington, D.C.: U.S. Government Printing Office, June 1999), 12; available from http://www.gao.gov/archive/1999/ns99136.pdf; Internet; accessed 19 February 2007.

[79] Douglas A. McVay, "Drug War Facts: Interdiction."

[80] Federal Bureau of Investigation, "Drug Offenders in the Corrections System," in *Crime in the United States – 1996*, Uniform Crime Reports (Washington, D.C.: U.S. Department of Justice, 1997), 62, Table 1.

[81] Russell F. Weigley, *The American Way of War* (Bloomington: Indiana University Press, 1973), xvii-xxiii.

[82] Perl, 2.

[83] Douglas A. McVay, "Drug War Facts: Economics," June 2005; available from http://www.drugwarfacts.org/economi.txt; Internet; accessed 4 February 2007.

[84] Jordan, "Same Drugs, Same Dangers."

www.ingramcontent.com/pod-product-compliance
Lightning Source LLC
Chambersburg PA
CBHW081808280526
45789CB00008B/3048

9 781500 284824